A Personal account of...

Time & Tide

Wells-next-the-Sea and Norfolk Coastal Floods, High Tides and Changes

by Janice Alamanou

With our own self belief we think that we might control nature's elements,
yet it is with disbelief that we see otherwise.

A Personal Account of... Time & Tide

Published by Janice Alamanou
For more copies of this book please contact:
JANICE ALAMANOU - COASTAL PHOTOGRAPHY
Gallery - 88 Staithe Street, Wells-next-the-Sea, Norfolk. NR23 1AQ
Telephone: 01328 712233
Mobile: 07798755757
E-mail: enquiries@coastalphotography.co.uk
Website: www.coastalphotography.co.uk

Designed and set by Janice Alamanou
Printed in Great Britain

Janice Alamanou's photographs are exhibited in UK
Galleries, Norfolk and London and throughout the year
2013/2014 in Florence, Italy. June 2014 her work was
exhibited at the Triennial exhibition of Visual Arts, in
Rome, Italy.

She is a member of the British Institute of Professional
Photography and has been awarded Gold and Merit
Awards for her landscapes from the BIPP.

The beginnings.......

As a young girl one of my first memories is on Wells-next-the-Sea beach on a cold January morning, a sharp wind biting into my face and frozen fingers grasping as I travelled along in my father's wheelbarrow. At that time my father was a fisherman with a boat in Wells-next-the-Sea harbour, but he also cast his nets on the foreshore which covered with the incoming tides and when the tide retreated, it unveiled a catch of a variety of fish. My father often took me with him on these cold winter days and my older brother, who would walk along beside us.

As I look back I can honestly say that the memory was more of immense disdain than any other emotion. The wind was so cold it made my face sting and my fingers had no feeling, I felt miserable. I moaned enough for the whole of Britain, I did not want to touch the fish or help get them into the barrow - why put your hands onto something colder than they already were? All the rants of a small child who would rather be in a warm, snug home with her toys. No reassurances of 'fresh air' or 'exercise', 'good for your lungs' or any other type of observance about 'the sand' or 'look at the colours on this fish' did any good. My mind was set - I wanted to go home and I would be unhappy (and in the process try to make everyone else unhappy) until I was home, especially as the way back usually meant walking as the wheelbarrow contained the fish.

This anecdote is now of great amusement to my father as a few years later I could not keep away from the beach, any beach for that matter, irrelevant to the weather, cold, wind, snow, storms and sunshine, I pulled on my boots and was off, running about the pinewood making dens with my friends, jumping over the marshlands and swimming in the creeks, not seeing a soul. Today things are very different, many more visitors to our beautiful coastline and the fishermen's nets are no longer cast. My father chuckles at the fact that those trips must have done something positive for me as natural landscape is now my passion, my work and a source of great sentiment. So, although I hated it on those particular days, in reality I can remember some days weren't quite so cold and there was often the odd shoulder ride home which I recall with great endearment.

At that young age was also the time that I was given my first camera, a 35mm film, point and shoot. I cannot remember the exact year only that it was much prior to my eighth birthday, a milestone of moving house onto the Quayside. Photography was a game to begin with, trying to 'snap' our big black dog named 'Chips' as he ran toward the camera and then trying to get him to sit still long enough to pose a reasonable shot. There were many blurred, unrecognizable images and lots of my brother with his head cut off, not literally of course but not getting the whole of him in the picture. After finishing the reel I would then dash to the chemist to get it developed and return, waiting eagerly to open the packet and see what I had. Sometimes opening immediately, over-eager and other times rushing home for the family to gather around and look at the results - every time there was a smile and we laughed - my joy of photography had begun.

Within a couple of years the two soon combined. On one of our trips my brother was helping my father with the nets, there was a bit of commotion and he pulled out an octopus. To us, this was an amazing event which I photographed on the quayside later while my brother proudly held up 'the catch' in his hands. The following day he took it to high school and it was placed in formaldehyde in the science room for everyone to see.

And so it began........

Time & Tide

The following series of photographs are a personal account of the devastating flood of 11th January 1978 that hit our coastline with great force. Following through the changes to the harbour, how the coasters used to visit and unload at the Quayside and the last time the funfair was on the Quay at Carnival time. Then to the destruction and magnitude of the flood of 5th December 2013. Again devastating a vast area of Norfolk coastline and how it has affected peoples homes and business. Showing images of Wells-next-the-Sea, Morston, Blakeney and Cromer.

Wells-next-the-Sea...

Wells-next-the-Sea...

Morston

Blakeney...

Cromer...

The morning after the flood
of January 1978.

Fishing boats and yachts all swept ashore from the volume of water that raised them over the wall and
onto the quayside. Wells-next-the-Sea.

The morning after the flood
of January 1978

Philip Platten sits in front of a local fishing boat raised onto the beach bank/sea defence by the flood the night before. The sea breached the bank, the water spilling through onto the fields and caravan site. Wells-next-the-Sea.

Time & Tide

January 11th 1978 Floods

As a twelve year old girl I witnessed one of the worst floods of the Norfolk coastline's history. At a time of high tides and matching winds the water surged its way up the channel, filling the harbour and covering the marshes with ferocious vigour. Our home then was the second floor flat on the Quayside, right in the middle and open to the elements. I remember our secondary double glazing began bending inward with the strength of the wind and my mother telling me to keep away from the windows, afraid that it would break. A promise that I did not keep as the curiosity to see something so different and unfamiliar urged me to go forward.

I noticed the fishermen first. In the storm, torrential rain and cold, they were wading through the water to the edge of the quay pushing their boats and holding them with all their strength as the waves slammed down, forcing them to crash against the wall. My father was one of them. The iciness of the North Sea in January, in the dark and coping with the force of the water as each and every one of them put their lives in danger, not knowing where the edge of the wall was exactly. One wrong footing and they could have gone down into the depths and crushed by their own boats or drowned in seconds from the cold sea. From my window I watched in fear as the men fought long and hard to save their vessels - their livelihoods.

The waves continued on, the sea rising fast, but we had another urgent problem. The ground floor of the building was the family business,we had a cafeteria combined with a bingo and arcade. If the sea was going to come in and it was already coming under thedoor, we had to move t he machines and stock fast. My father was torn. At heart, was and always is, his boat, but his head made him leave. He placed scaffolding poles to try to hold his vessel in his absence. At this point we were all downstairs. We worked hard, my father and brother lifting and dragging the slot machines, pinball, juke box, fridges and electrical equipment to the rear of the building up three steps to a higher level and all of us carrying the stock. Police were outside ushering people away as many had come to watch but it was becoming dangerous. The fishermen had to abandon their boats by this time and watched defeated as they rose over and on top of the wall, waves beating them back and forth. My father's boats had bent the scaffolding and slid over the top. A large coaster that had come into harbour to unload grain and moored at the Quay was rising fast and began tilting over the wall edge too. I had no boots and the water was becoming deeper inside the building, the cold biting into my skin. We couldn't do much more, so much stock, but the force and speed of the water was immense. It was up to my knees in a short time and still we were lifting and piling things high. The coaster had lifted and sat on the quayside rolling as the waves crashed into it's side. Although for some, this acted as a break between the storm and their buildings. We had to stop and retreat upstairs to safety as the waves were crashing against our doorway and hitting the canopy above. We reluctantly gave in, tired and cold and listened to a long night of howling winds and raging waters.

The following morning was calm. An early morning revealed the devastation of the previous night. At first glance out of the window I saw all the fishing boats on the car park of the Quay. The coaster, the Function, slightly further along - everywhere covered in seaweed. Then to my horror I saw that the main beach bank sea defence had breached and the water had rushed through, taking fishing boats with it. One remained on top of the bank, another was all the way over the road and onto the children's play area. Sea water remained all over the fields, the sluices not able to deal with the drainage, water as far as I could see. It is a sight I will never forget.

We went downstairs to look at our building. On the ground floor the doors were closed and yet seaweed lay on the floor. All the floor was damaged, the wood parquet lifted and strewn everywhere. Water and the damp smell, everything sodden. Further along the quayside shop windows had smashed completely and the water had rushed in and swept everything away. We had been lucky. The coaster had taken the brunt of the waves and protected a few buildings behind it. People were starting to mill about, coming to look at the devastation. My father went to inspect the damage to his boats - alongside the other fishermen.

That day was one of mixed feelings, a day of sorrow and loss for so many along our coast but also a time for some of us to count our blessings, however small, and move forward.

The morning after the flood
of January 1978.

The beach bank breached and water still flooding the fields and caravan site. Fishing boats were swept through and deposited onto the fields and play areas.

My brother proudly showing his catch of an octopus
caught in my father's nets on the foreshores of the beach.

This was later displayed at the Alderman Peel High School
and pupils had access to see and learn about octopi and sea life.

The last days of the adult rides of the funfair being allowed onto the quayside at Carnival. Summer 2000. Wells-next-the-Sea.

A band in the parade. Last days of the funfair on the quayside at Carnival. Summer 2000. Wells-next-the-Sea.

Floats ride by. The last of the main rides of the funfair allowed on the Quay at Carnival. Wells-next-the-Sea.

Coaster and old barge moored at the quayside. The crane parked, ready for unloading. Wells-next-the-Sea.

Time & Tide

Changes...

Through the years Wells-next-the-Sea has had it's changes. I remember the harbour being almost straight at low tide and still passable for small boats. A very vague memory of hydro-plane racing and of course the coasters that used to come into this busy working port to unload their grain and meal. The harbour's pilot boat would escort them down the channel to their moorings at the wall, where the cranes were permanently sat at the ready. Poles were created along the car park edge, inside the small wall, for large sheets to be erected to stop the produce from blowing into the shops and onto the pavements opposite. The lorries would come and the cranes lifted the load into the truck to be transported. Many different ships came and went, usually staying only 2 or 3 days at a time. From my 'birds eye view' window I often watched as the men worked hard, getting ready to unload and then arms waving to direct the crane driver to where he needed to place the crane head inside the ship's hull.

Another set of workers I watched came very rarely to Wells, only once a year for a few days. These were the people from the travelling funfair. Although a few still come to the town each Carnival, the last time they had big rides on the Quayside was the year 2000. Until then it was expected that Carnival time would mean the fair on the Quay. People enjoyed the music and the rides swinging out over the harbour, making them feel more dangerous and exciting. I liked some of them but what really entertained me the most was the putting up and disassembling of the machinery. I watched as they put blocks to level the ground and steady the equipment. They worked swiftly and hard to quickly arrange all the rides and stalls to be ready to open - three days open meant one day to assemble and on the Sunday, at finish of Carnival, they would take it all down, working into the night so when I got up early the next morning there was nothing there to see.

It quickly changed from a hectic weekend to a still busy, but more tranquil environment. The swans could be seen as they glided through the water and the fishing boats lined the wall, their colours brightening the day. In previous years when my father had his boats, the fishermen caught fish and would sit on the Quayside mending their nets. They would go out on the tide and had their own whistles on the radio to identify and communicate who was who at sea. I would sit on the edge of the wall and wait for his boat to come in on the returning tide and see what he had caught. A little easier to the days when I had to go to the beach for his nets.

The beaches have also altered, with the amount of visitors but also with the build up of sand in our area, even though for many along the coast it is completely the opposite with extreme erosion of the cliffs and shoreline which is clearly visible going toward and past Cromer and in the other direction at Hunstanton. Houses and caravan sites on the edge as cliffs erode, land fall of metres at a time.

Change always happens. The harbour still has it's work boats - the tankers were eventually replaced by the wind farm boats as the harbour silted up over time and there was not enough depth for the boats to come in. At low tide the once straight channel now becomes a meandering shallow stream. The windfarm needs quick access to their boats which meant an expansion of a new internal harbour at the sea-end of the town. The fishing fleet still line the Quayside and bring home their catch to the awe of tourists and locals alike - only now they catch crabs, lobsters and shrimps instead of fish. The 'Show' must always go on and the Carnival is no exception with new events and activities and as always the floats. Even the funfair still comes, albeit in a different place and not as large as I remember, erected beside the football pitch. My greatest 'miss' are there are no longer any swans. To watch them float by, gracefully and serene, used to be a daily pleasure. Today the harbour is full with geese and ducks, plus many different species of coastal birds, but I still yearn for the swans to return.

When coasters and cranes were common place. The poles in the background were erected to hold sheeting. This would be used to stop some of the grain and meal from blowing into the shops and on the pavements the other side of the road. Wells-next-the-Sea.

A very normal sight years ago was an abundance of swans in the harbour. I would look forward to seeing them every day and miss their majestic presence frequenting the banks and water of the quay. Wells-next-the-Sea.

The fishing fleet line the wall of the harbour. A sight still seen today but without the swans and endless people that enjoyed throwing a piece of bread. Unfortunately this became a danger to them as they would confuse a possible piece of food with the bait of people crabbing (gillying to the natives) with hooks off of the wall. The hooks were banned and the crabbing continues. Wells-next-the-Sea.

High tides of 2007. Dismounting from the Albatros. Not in danger at all as this was merely a spring tide, but a humourous photograph as he didn't want to get his feet wet. Wells-next-the-Sea.

High Spring Tides of 2007. The Albatros at the side of the Quay wall, water flooding over the car park. No immediate danger with this tide. Wells-next-the-Sea.

Time & Tide

5th December 2013 Flood

Wells-next-the-Sea and the Norfolk coast had endured two major floods , 1953 and 1978, with 25 years between. From then, there had been occasional high tides that would crawl up the car park but nothing that could be recognized as potentially dangerous - apart from the odd car that had been left on the car park while the owners were enjoying the town, only to return and the wheels were immersed in water. This is more a regularity along at Blakeney and in the other direction at Burnham Overy Staithe. So when the Environment Agency issued a warning of a sea surge that would flood on 5th December 2013, 35 years on, it seemed almost surreal. I no longer live on the Quay but my building that used to be the family business is still open with tenants running their own business. Through the day, boards and sand bags were erected all the way along the front, with people trying to barricade their properties from the threat of water. The morning was calm weather, the wind offshore and the threat of the waves of 1978 didn't seem likely. Local men talked about the conditions and whether the wind would keep the water off. Everything was in place to protect, it was just a matter of waiting. High tide was predicted at 8pm.

At 6.15pm my daughter rushed from her bedroom, "You'd better get down there mum, the water is really high. It's already on the internet." Having lived through the previous flood all I can say is, as many more who have been affected by floods must feel - the feeling of doom that begins in your stomach and begins to grow. I walked down Jicklings Yard to begin with. It was 6.30pm and very dark. The water was too high for me to pass with my wellington boots on. I could not even get to the Quayside to check my building. I went back up and around to Staithe Street. People were milling about, crowds were forming. The sea had consumed the back of the pub and was lapping it's way up the road. At this point I could do nothing but hope. There was a spark and the mains electric went off. I decided to walk back around the town to the other side of the sea defence wall so that I might get a better view of my building.

From this point it was clear to me that this flood was higher than the last, although the wind was still offshore and there were no waves in the harbour, the speed at which the sea was rising was only to be believed with your own eyes. The environment agency and the press were there. Crowds of people, some climbing on the wall to get better pictures. By this time the level of water had risen to the glass panelling above the wall and the sea was trying to force it's way through the seams, spilling onto the pavement and beginning to flood the road the other side. It was becoming apparent that it could be catastrophically dangerous if the wall were to give way. The volume of water it was containing was immense. The Environment Agency and the police began moving people back and cordoning the area off. I walked back along to Staithe Street.

It was in Staithe Street that I was told my doors had just given way. People everywhere, some watching in awe, some giggling - many different emotions. I stood as if the world was going on around me. I knew that the force of that water breaking the door would then crash through my building like a tsunami. I walked to Standard Road.

I was not alone. Here I met with friends that had been forced from their homes. The sea had claimed them. The Chandlers on the corner of Standard Road sits in a slight dip on the Quayside and the water was deep inside. They had little hope. I could only imagine the homes and businesses along the coast that must have been severely hit. So far, we didn't know of any casualties to life.

Before the flood of 5th December 2013. Sandbags and wooden barracades in the Quay car park entrance. Usually enough to hold the sea at bay Wells-next-the-Sea.

Floods - 5th December 2013. The water rose so quickly but compared to the 1978 floods, the wind was offshore and the water was relatively calm in this area. With the amount of devastation to the town without the onshore wind, we were thankful for small mercies. Wells-next-the-Sea.

Floods - 5th December 2013. All the mains electricity for the buildings up to the Granary had cut off. Wells-next-the-Sea.

Floods - 5th December 2013. People stood on the flood defence wall, the water reaching the glass panelling. The pressure from the quantity of water was immense, but the wall held. Wells-next-the-Sea.

Floods - 5th December 2013. The strain of holding back the sea surge begins to show as the sea defence wall starts to leak along the seams. Wells-next-the-Sea.

Floods - 5th December 2013. The sea defence wall could have breached. The water level reaching the glass, the sheer quantity and force against the wall made the water force through any available seams. Sandbags were placed to stop as much as possible and people were cleared back by the environment agency. Wells-next-the-Sea.

Floods - 5th December 2013. Locals line the road opposite the flood defence wall. The sea, by that time, spilling from the wall and reaching across the road. Wells-next-the-Sea.

Floods - 5th December 2013. Up Standard Road the water continues to surge. A lone yacht remains secure in the background. Wells-next-the-Sea.

Floods - 5th December 2013. The sea gets higher and higher as the waves gently roll forward. Wells-next-the-Sea.

Time & Tide

And still the water rose further. Gentle but swift in her determination, Mother Nature pushed her element of water further toward the town. No one could get to the Quayside at this point without a boat. A lone yacht could be seen by the Chandlery in Standard Road steadfast on it's mooring. In Staithe Street the waves slowly edged further up, passing the Golden Fleece. By this time, the Quayside in darkness. The car park coin machines sparked and fused, followed by all the electicity in the buildings. Only lights from the Granary and the Albatros allowed a view to the destruction and enormity of this tide.

Flood of 5th December 2013. The highest recorded flood water in Wells-next-the-Sea. High tide due at 8pm, this photograph was taken around 6.30pm. Already the water was too deep to reach the Quay with wellington boots on. Wells-next-the-Sea.

Floods - 5th December 2013. The sea level pushed the water up Staithe Street and many of the buildings were flooded from the rear. Wells-next-the-Sea.

Floods - 5th December 2013. Local people watch in disbelief as the water continues to rise and they are forced from their homes. Wells-next-the-Sea.

Floods - 5th December 2013. The street signs are nearly immersed. Wells-next-the-Sea.

Floods - 5th December 2013. One of the buildings that was consumed by the highest water, the Chandlery had little hope of staying dry. Wells-next-the-Sea.

Floods - 5th December 2013. The Quay from Standard Road. Only the street lights and the Granary lights remained.
Wells-next-the-Sea.

Floods - 5th December 2013. Local people watch in awe as still the water rises up Standard Road. Wells-next-the-Sea.

Time & Tide

5th December 2013 Flood continued...

When the flood water started to recede it was visible that the wooden blocks between the quayside central car park entrance had broken and become debris in the sea. The sand bags were strewn and the beginning of the devastation could be seen. Many of the buildings had water completely inside, for some their sand bags had held at the front and the water had gone in from a back door. On inspection of my own building, I saw that the water had completely consumed the building. Large ice cream fridges had been carried half way down the building and cast onto their sides. Electronic arcade machines were filled with water - all destroyed. The water level had reached the back of the building. A sight I had never seen and a clear indication that this was the highest level - at least in my time. Was it because of the volume of water or because the sea defence wall re-directed it toward the main area of town? In 1978, the bank breached and the water flooded to the fields, yet still we had water inside the building. Thankfully a part of the town was protected. Thankfully also, that the wind remained offshore. The tall ship raised a sail to help keep it from floating onto the Quayside and for the rest, the lack of waves reduced the destruction to the buildings.

Within the following week amongst the sorting of the building repairs and trying to come to terms with this type of 'loss', I took trips to see the beach and other parts of the coast. My first stop was Wells-next-the-Sea beach. The beach I grew up on, so many memeories and a part of my soul. The first thing I noticed was that the new outer harbour seemed ok. I walked over by the Coastwatch hut and saw weed and grasses all over the top of the walkway and on the ends of the groynes. The lifeboat was standing outside the Lifeboat House and I was informed that many tonnes of debris had to be removed from inside as they had to open the front and back doors of the house in order for it to stay standing. Along this area, as well as other parts of the coast, there were waves. The beach huts at the beginning were gone. The first five - only a couple of legs were left. Further along many had been taken completely and several that remained were badly damaged or unsafe. The sand had been carved by the sea into shelves by the huts and as I walked toward the main dune further out I could see a strata effect in the sand as the sea had cut huge portions of the dune away, leaving what looked like a cliff face. What had once been a sandy area for children to run up and roll down was, at this stage, a steep, sheer edge.

Over days of visitors and people climbing, along with wind and tides, this reduced down to a smooth surface, albeit smaller, once again. With all things, nature's elements change things and surprise us and then fill us with happiness yet again.

Floods - 5th December 2013. As the sea retreats sandbags are washed through the open car park entrance, previously filled with boards and sandbags that were broken and swept away. Wells-next-the-Sea.

After the Flood - December 2013. Pontoons swept onto the Quay. The tide retreated and returned, still hgh the following morning, covering the marsh.Wells-next-the-Sea.

After the Flood - December 2013. The morning of 6th December. Maintenance vans line the quayside Many of the buildings with water inside and assessing the damage begins. Wells-next-the-Sea.

After the Flood - December 2013. Broken beach huts strewn onto the beach bank..Wells-next-the-Sea.

After the Flood - December 2013. Beach huts broken and wood drifted onto the dunes. The first five huts completely demolished. Many others gone or damaged.Wells-next-the-Sea.

After the Flood - December 2013. Weed and grasses are strewn over the walkway boards and on top of the ends of the groynes. Wells-next-the-Sea.

After the Flood - December 2013. Debris carried by the sea surge ends up knitted onto the walk way. The Lifeboat House in the background, reportedly had many tonnes of debris to remove from the interior. The men worked hard to ensure minimum damage - a valuable service we could not do without in these parts. Wells-next-the-Sea.

After the Flood - December 2013. Beach huts destroyed and swept into the sea. Wells-next-the-Sea.

After the Flood - December 2013. For many only steps still stand. The beach huts were torn apart. Wells-next-the-Sea.

After the Flood - December 2013. Those beach huts that remain are mostly damaged. You can imagine the force of the water to do this much destruction. Wells-next-the-Sea.

After the Flood - December 2013. The change in the level of the sand as the sea cut, leaving a clear shelf in the dune. Wells-next-the-Sea.

After the Flood - December 2013. Battered beach huts with sand swept and cut under and around them. Wells-next-the-Sea.

After the Flood - December 2013. The dunes that protect the beach, the interior dunes and the beach huts were carved as though they were butter. Very little of the original width and height of sand is left. Wells-next-the-Sea.

After the Flood - December 2013. Safety netting surrounds damaged Beach Huts. Wells-next-the-Sea.

After the Flood - December 2013. Posts are put in place to hold the unstable beach huts as the legs have been wrenched out of place. Wells-next-the-Sea.

After the Flood - December 2013.
By the steps, covered in sand, used to be a beach hut. Just an empty space remains. Wells-next-the-Sea.

After the Flood - December 2013. Sand is carved into a ledge before the beach huts. Others have had the sand swept by the surge from their steps, but only time will tell if it will build up again. Wells-next-the-Sea.

After the Flood - December 2013. Fallen beach huts. Wells-next-the-Sea.

After the Flood - December 2013. The beginning of the beach huts. The first five were completely swept away, only the odd footing pole stands. It was difficult to define whose was whose as the remnants of wood are collected and cleared. Wells-next-the-Sea.

After the Flood - December 2013. Below the Coastwatch hut the metal girder was bent and pushed from the sea defence. Wells-next-the-Sea.

5th December Floods continued...

A few days later I drove along the coast toward Blakeney. The clear-up was under way, tractors scooped up weed and debris from the roads, debris that had come through the breached banks protecting the villages. The water had surged, cutting through soil and grass, shingle and pebbles, taking everything in it's path and sweeping it all the way to the village. The water had not retreated by this time and was still deep on the fields. For some wildlife this was fatal, for others - a new residence.

At Morston the bridges were broken down and access to the marsh and boats was limited.

As I drove down to Blakeney harbour, a yacht stranded on the top of the bank was the first evidence of the height the water had reached. A second vessel lay stranded by one of the breaches. There were many gapping holes in the coastal path along the sea defence bank that stretches all the way along this part of the coast. I parked the car and tried to walk along the path. It was extremely wet and I could get no further than the car park area before having to climb down to go around the large gaping holes.

Many of the homes and businesses of Blakeney were flooded and people were clearing and sorting their premises, just as they had been in Wells. Just as they were all along the coast.

After the Flood - December 2013. Along the coast at Morston. The bridge over the salt marsh broken down from the sea surge.
Morston.

After the Flood - December 2013. The calm after the storm. The boarding and rails of the bridge completely gone. Morston.

After the Flood - December 2013. Further along the coast the banks were breached completely and the sea still remains on the surrounding fields. The boats were thrown from their moorings, this one landing on the car park area of the bank. Blakeney.

After the Flood - December 2013. The breached banks, this was only the beginning. Many areas all the way along are like this and worse. People try to walk and see how far they can go along their normal coastal path. The soil was very wet. Blakeney.

After the Flood - December 2013. Looking back from the bank toward the town. A field normally for cattle and wildlife is now covered in sea water. Blakeney.

After the Flood - December 2013. The breached bank and the curiousity of the boat on the bank. Blakeney.

Time & Tide

5th December Flood continued...

I travelled further along the coast toward Cromer, passing through Salthouse where the banks, visible from the road, were destroyed in many places and again cleaning up was in process.

As I approached the front at Cromer I noticed that large chunks of the concrete sea defence wall had been destroyed. Men were working hard clearing the debris into skips extremely quickly. The Pier had planks ripped from the deck, but still stood firm. I stopped to speak to one of the workers, a Scottish man who was repairing the Pier. He told me that the most damage was at the near-end as the far-end had more recently been renovated and was stronger. They were working to make a walkway along one side of the Pier so that the Theatre could be opened by that weekend. Only one week after the flood - and it did open at that time.

I walked further down the beach toward the beach huts. They were battered, bashed and knocked. I could not see one visible that I believed could be salvagable. Wood lay on the beach, the huts tilted over, many missing and all broken. Cromer does not have a channel and is open to the elements, so the waves here must have been frighteningly destructive. This confirmed by the amount of concrete that had been ripped away.

After the Flood - December 2013. Cromer beach huts. This area of the coastline had no channel to difuse the surge, which created waves that pounded the shore. Beach huts were smashed by the force. Cromer.

After the Flood - December 2013. Some beach huts remain, but battered and broken. Cromer.

After the Flood - December 2013. The beach huts are destroyed. Cromer.

After the Flood - December 2013. Just wooden debris lines the promenade. Cromer.

After the Flood - December 2013. Broken beach huts to the pier. Cromer.

After the Flood - December 2013. People walk the beach to view the damage. Cromer.

After the Flood - December 2013. The force of the water is clear as the remains of the beach huts lay thrown and smashed by the waves. Cromer.

After the Flood - December 2013. The beach is clear of debris but the beach huts lay tattered before the pier. Cromer.

After the Flood - December 2013. Repairs to Cromer Pier get quickly underway. The end of the pier not being hit as severely as the beginning. Planks of wood were stripped, leaving the deck bare with holes to the sea below. Cromer.

Time & Tide

Cyan ripples, a whispering hush on the shore
Bare soles sinking, warm granules enfold
Hearts open as light tingles the skin
Spirits drift the breeze as summer begins

Haliards chime, ringing the changing wind
Cool greens and greys lick the Quay
Blue canvas colours the darkening marsh
As warm fire fingers beckon from within
Our minds quieten as winter begins

Swift sea surges, to battle commence
Nature lashes her watery whip
Her icy grip is searching our land
Torment wields, then she leaves in peace
Changing time and tide, as a new day begins.

by Janice Alamanou

THE END